The Glass Globe

POEMS

The Glass Globe

Margaret Gibson

LOUISIANA STATE UNIVERSITY PRESS

Baton Rouge

Published by Louisiana State University Press
lsupress.org

LSU Press Paperback Original

Designer: Mandy McDonald Scallan
Typeface: Adobe Caslon Pro

Cover photograph of flowers by Chrissa Giannakoudi/unsplash

Thanks to the following journals where these poems were previously published:

American Journal of Poetry (online): "Grace," "Mountain Koan," and "Slowly"; *Connecticut River Review:* "Reflection, Looking Straight Ahead"; *Connecticut Woodlands*: "Star Koan"; *Georgia Review:* "Like so Much Weather" (as "Negative Capability") and "Resilience"; *Gettysburg Review:* "Asides and Notations," "The Glass Globe," "Intimacy," "Irrevocable" "The Keep," "One Hour," "Panang Curry with Shrimp and Gustav Sobin," "Scrolls," and "Solving for the Root"; *Here:* "Deliberate and a Little Stern," "Greed," and "Long Division"; *Image:* "Judge Not," "Riverkeeper," and "What He Knew"; *Michigan Quarterly Review:* "Washing the Body"; *Mountain Record:* "Always an Immigrant"; *Southern Review:* "Wing"; and *Where the River Bends, An Anthology:* "Waiting." "Irrevocable" also appeared in *Waking Up to the Earth: Connecticut Poets in a Time of Global Climate Crisis.*

Library of Congress Cataloging-in-Publication Data
Names: Gibson, Margaret, 1944– author.
Title: The glass globe : poems / Margaret Gibson.
Description: Baton Rouge : Louisiana State University Press, [2021] | "LSU
    Press Paperback Original"—Title page verso.
Identifiers: LCCN 2020052729 (print) | LCCN 2020052730 (ebook) | ISBN
    978-0-8071-7563-7 (paperback) | ISBN 978-0-8071-7589-7 (pdf) | ISBN
    978-0-8071-7590-3 (epub)
Subjects: LCGFT: Poetry.
Classification: LCC PS3557.I1916 G53 2021 (print) | LCC PS3557.I1916
    (ebook) | DDC 811/.54—dc23
LC record available at https://lccn.loc.gov/2020052729
LC ebook record available at https://lccn.loc.gov/2020052730

This book is for David, who walked gently on the Earth.

Contents

Washing the Body • 1

○

How It Is • 5
Moment • 6
Panang Curry with Shrimp and Gustav Sobin • 8
Long Division • 11
Grief and the Art of Archery • 13
Waiting • 17
Scrolls • 19
Mountain Koan • 21
Slowly • 22
Deliberate and a Little Stern • 24
Looking Back, Looking Now • 26
What He Knew • 28

○

The Glass Globe • 35

○

Riverkeeper • 39
Resilience • 41
Reflection, Looking Straight Ahead • 45
Greed • 48
Asides and Notations • 49
Sky Pond Place • 53
Cloud Koan • 56
Solving for the Root • 58
Butternut Squash Heart Sutra • 59

White Phlox • 62

Like So Much Weather • 64

Because the Earth • 68

○

Exchange • 73

○

Wing • 79

Judge Not • 85

Never Pitiless Enough or Kind • 88

The Keep • 90

When Everything Broken Is Broken • 92

One Hour • 94

Star Koan • 96

This Morning • 98

Tiger, Tiger • 100

Intimacy • 101

Grace • 103

Always an Immigrant • 104

○

Irrevocable • 109

Notes • 117

The Glass Globe

WASHING THE BODY

And last, we washed his body

Last, we rolled it to one side of the bed, rocked it gently back, the long
        length of him settled now onto a clean sheet

Last, I followed a crease on his forehead with my finger

Last, his daughter washed his hair, massaging his scalp, sloshing
        the soapy water

Last, his son sponged his shoulders

And I, each finger; he had beautiful hands

Last, his thighs, his knees, his shin blades

Last, we washed his feet, their soles a smooth new silk

And I for the last time his genitals, still warm as a woods-earth nestle
        of wild orchid

His no-breath-now stayed sweet

Last, his eyebrows, bushy, outrageous, a fleck of water caught there
        bright in the lamplight, as if a snowflake from a walk we took
        years back across a white field had freshly fallen

I don't know who crossed his arms across his chest

And last, he was warm when I kissed a mouth that would not close
        nor speak, nor allow us to enter

the mystery of his being beyond us now, no crossing that threshold

And the silence in the room was, as it always is, ordinary and vast

HOW IT IS

...and in the long sigh of the outbreath, his last
I pull on a sweater

In the long sigh of the outbreath
I wash a spoon

I put on my shoes

In the long sigh of the outbreath, his last
I open the door
close the door

my hand lingering on the round brass knob

I have a new way now of measuring time

In the long sigh of the outbreath, his last
I read a book
watch the news

turn the garden

boil water ... and it is stunning to boil water

just to see it ripple out the faucet at first
the same as it used to

In the long sigh of the outbreath, his last
I am dying
I'm already dead, and I'm alive

breathing in the long sigh of the outbreath
his last

and I still cannot, even now, believe
(in the long, long sigh of the outbreath, his last)

how intimate it is, how sweet

MOMENT

When your eyes suddenly opened, I brought my face closer
turned into breath
                    and slid into your throat

just as a sigh of outbreath, your last, carried you back to what you'd never left—
        brooks and forests

rocks and deer trails, steep fields, stars, and the dark matter no one notices

And you became the impulse a wood thrush yields to, singing . . .
became once again
                    the slow spread of moss and lichen on granite

once again, the ancestors—men who blew on their hands in winter, women who
        pressed grapes

into wine for communion and festival, children at play in the yard

And although time
is an onslaught
                we live

equally in the inbreath of oceans and in the outbreath of mountains
as they turn
                into ravine and valley and field

It is always just one moment we inhabit

Birds that live on a golden mountain reflect the color of the gold

Just so, when we married, I crossed the room, I walked toward you
                and you took my face into your hands

according to the ancient compact of earth and sun . . . and the original brightness
        of that moment

is the original brightness of this, that day was this day

and we said, *yes* . . . we said, yes . . .

December 27, 2017
December 27, 1975

PANANG CURRY WITH
SHRIMP AND GUSTAF SOBIN

(If only ...)
              as Panang curry

in a round dish, onto the white cloth
set down gently

offered

So many colors mingling in a fragrant sauce
from which appear

(he has been dead two months now)

geologic peaks of rice

and also, these
faintly
saline
involuted
sea creatures
              pink and white, each for all the world

a muted
vocable
or
    a musical note about to unfurl

(the sense of hearing is the last to go)

about to unfurl, yes

as Sobin says

like so much weather
out of the west, sound arrives with its
scooped
hollows, the caves it makes in

the very midst of

mass

Even so, and even if
only

temporary, music

arrives as a flavor
of sound

arrives, each

tocsin, toccata, or descant
of
air
in-
canted

in-gathered ... and released

(tell how you want to die)
(tell also how you want to live)

and, even if only for an instant

that single chord
with its particular tang and timbre

(both hands on the keyboard now
as in Saint-Saëns)

would be enough
                                    yes: gathered

sound as signature, resounding

even if

wafted, now, on
ever

more
tenuous
frequencies

(I can still hear his voice)

Absence as presence: irrevocable, and yet

a full life to savor, yes

LONG DIVISION

. . . as if grief were commensurable

as if it would agree
to be reckoned

I divide the sum of my life so far
by your death

And I keep going, I divide
mountain
        by a train whistle
        tremulous in the night

Owl call
        by the way you used to
        say my name

River
        by the hymn I haven't
        sung for years

Cedars at dusk
        by rainlight I locked
        inside a box
        then lost the key

The road ahead
        by the number of breaths
        it will take me
        to travel it

And silence
        immeasurable silence

by the loose change
my hand finds

cool to the touch

in the pocket of a coat
you left behind in the closet

GRIEF AND THE ART OF ARCHERY

○

Younger, alive
in what now seems another life

and grieving for we knew not what
we used to argue

Who knew how sharp the arrow
or if
      the wound might heal

Oh, but we were civil!

There was strategy
and plea

Conviction. Truce without
mercy
      Then we'd cheat

and move the target

○

*In the case of archery, the hitter and the hit are no longer two opposing objects
but are one reality.*

○

"Of course, the relationship continues," replies a friend
whose husband
            has also died

If the words sound too easy, they are not
meant as final, only

a moment's refuge

before the ground caves
and becomes
bottomless

a black pool
no one truly believes is there beneath us

○

All along, we are afloat
on this pool

When we argued
we ruffled the surface

We feathered it, we rowed
this way and that

Or, icebound, we waited

Zen says, "Empty boat"
But we wanted

to feel passion's friction
and release

"Love is the goal of argument"
we agreed

The heart—pierced by an arrow

○

*"Your arrows do not carry," observed the Master," because they do not reach
far enough . . . You must act as if the goal were infinitely far off."*

○

In the afterlife of dreams

I discover the two of us
still in argument

still trying to reach past
obstacle
and the desire to change each other

All night we argue, the words at times
oddly sweet

After death, you'd think the rules
would change

The rules never change, and the target

moves

○

The grief that shields itself
with argument

and shies from notice
is as steep as the crest of the hill

where, summers, we'd sit, finally
able to yield

without speaking, without touching
as the valley blued

and shifted through the shadow graph
of clouds to river sound

and stars. We'd listen. There's an art
to listening to the stars

And when we could sense
a stillness at the heart of things

we'd walk through it, home

○

Steep is the way to mastery . . .

○

Things change, standing still . . .

There comes a slip of light
through which
               the arrow may fly

and hit the heart of the moment

Touching an arrow to the tip of my tongue
raising the bow in stillness . . .

In this darkness, there is
no waiting

and no one who waits. No one
to practice
           no one to grieve

The hand opens. Straight and sure, the arrow
is drawn
        and released

by its target

○

It is all so simple. You can learn from an ordinary bamboo leaf what ought to happen. It bends lower and lower under the weight of snow. Suddenly the snow slips to the ground without the leaf having stirred.

WAITING

...and just now I'm tired of waiting, yes, I admit it as readily
as the north window admits
yellow light
the sun going down behind the maples
a primal gold
that deepens
to amber, the lampshade by the window table
also amber
a few more hours to go
before I close the book
take tea
and try to sleep
Now sky is rose and indigo, and the books
on their steep shelves
have slipped into shadow
reticent, even
shy
now their collective wisdoms no longer daunt
What little I know
I know
Yet any moment now a desolate
sere, and utterly
lovely
upsurge of wind
which is also the sound of my letting my breath out slow
may offer
the word I've been listening for each evening
listening perhaps
because a long time ago now I asked to be given it, I asked
to be able to receive it
what the word actually feels like, and is—
forgiven...
                    but the word-forge is hidden in the heart
no telling what sets it going or how long
the fires burn

although in truth there is no forge
no fire, no self
to smelt, or mint, or make anew ... perhaps
just the asking
is enough
the gasp of breath, what it takes
to ask, enough—

        the very thought makes my heart beat faster

SCROLLS

Where did they go, the long winter months
after . . . I remember staring at my shoes
I remember cups of tea. I remember
carrying wood for the fire, and long walks
with our dog to Main Brook, which didn't
freeze this winter. You'd remember the years
it did. Po Chu-i, or was it Li Po, wrote
I wake at midnight and sit up straight in bed
I do that, too, and sometimes pull on my coat
and go outside and stand beneath the stars
In the morning, it's as if the stars go out
but they don't; they don't, and today
it's spring. The red-winged blackbirds flash
I hear dove-call in the cedars. I've set
the pots of amaryllis into south-window light
and their bud-tips like Chinese brushes
rise up out of the squat bulbs, their color
deepens. The jar that holds your ashes
I've put in an east window, where the moon
can find it at night. *The moon, alas, is*
no drinker of wine . . . I still sit
facing the chair you used to pull nearer
the fire. Orion has shifted further
west, soon it will slip over the horizon
the Dipper balances on its handle
the nights are long. But I said that. Red
streaks the sky, come dawn, and reminds me
of the flush in your skin. Even so
there will come at least a day when I don't
think of you—I want to say it isn't fair
it isn't just, but you'd be the first to remind
that easy-to-get guns aren't just, pigs
at the trough aren't just, nor are refugee camps
amputations, self-pity, inattention
opioids—one could go on and on. Like you

I continue to read the Chinese poets
who governed cities, got sick, then withdrew
into the mountains to wait for the moon
drink wine, write . . . returning to fame
profit, and dust. In a dream, you sat up
and smiled at me. You were young again
Your hair was brown. I will suppose therefore
that sunset and sunrise are just, that poems
which begin in illness and idleness
then open the heart, are just; also just
these shadows of branches on the late March snow—
as lovely as brush strokes on silken scrolls
they will last as long as deep quiet
lasts, whose ravines and waterfalls and mists
unroll and unroll, the scrolls so lengthy
one might think they'd go on forever . . .

MOUNTAIN KOAN

Where does one go from the summit
of the mystic mountain?

Coming down mountain, I remember other questions
that once broke my heart—
Where did everybody go?

and, after I told him I loved him, *Why?*

the moment so sharp-shorn not even love

could pick the lock
to his solitary confinement—that's what the mind with Alzheimer's

is, at times
Oddly, not unlike

the everyday hazy mind that only knows
being other than
mountains and rivers and the great wide earth

Coming down mountain
mountain

abides—now

a white-capped stone I carry in my pocket, now

a poem as much like granite as it can be

now mountain heartbeat, high and broad, riding the clouds

SLOWLY

Slowly I'm making my way
to a single life, a life
someday I'll want to call *new*...
but there still are snow crusts
in the yard, and in the shade
of the stone wall you built, stiff
crests of it
          It's hard, it's cold—
is this a weather report?
A progress report? *Have we
arrived yet,* asks a small voice
that wants pain deferred...
and it's true, I'd prefer to be
walking the narrow ridge
with you mornings in the town
where you grew up
              where it snowed
record amounts in winter
and firs in the thick spring woods
gave off their strange pungency
and I don't like it, I don't
like going ahead *without*—
a quick glance over my shoulder
a glimpse all that's left of the
summers we spent in the midst of
memories you'd harbored—
you can't go home again
but you did
          and from a hill
that overlooked the worn-out town
you described the quiet mornings
you'd ventured into the snow
before anyone else, and
it was wholly yours—the town
the world

Almost, I could touch
the boy in you . . . And what if
I'd been able to love the iron in you
that was your father's ghost?
We did our best to heal each other
and it wasn't hindsight's
distant squint that soothed, and not
our words that brought new life
I put down my pen—what more
is there to say? I can be
still. I can wait, alone
on the stone bench in the yard
however long, in any weather, any
light. Ready
now for you to touch me again
in silence, *as* silence . . .

DELIBERATE AND A LITTLE STERN

Still and bare as a moon
you live in my mind, rising there in the evenings

sloping down the sky into the oaks by morning

I have a sense of your presence
that at times has felt like a hand touching lightly

the small of my back

But if you could return to life for a moment
and sit near, you'd have questions

and they wouldn't be about me

Even late in your illness, you'd watch
the hollow-eyed children on the news

I hate this, you'd say, *but I have to see it*

I imagine you sitting beside me
deliberate and a little stern

Leaning in close, you want to know

how many children now are hungry
in the midst of famines our government

sanctions. How many

cross to an imagined safe haven and are
swept from rafts into the sea

And the flies, count them

how many are still crawling over the eyelids
of children left behind in the camps

Closer to home, how much blood

is spilled in cop cars, on street corners
in school rooms? How many

children will it take ... how many guns

How many yachts, oil rigs, and earrings
to distract us from those without

medicine or shelter or food

It's winter. You know all about winter
I hear your voice, hoarse and insistent, rise

from the Bardo of spirits who, like you

once intimate with arid despair, still bless us
unawares—we who need blessing

more than we know

Blessed are the poor in spirit, you remind me
holding out your hands. How empty

they are ... even as they fill with light

LOOKING BACK, LOOKING NOW

Long before your illness became apparent, I think you knew
you were dying, even in the midst of life, dying, as we all are . . .

Dying. I say it easily now. Back then, I embraced the usual
distractions, and I think you grieved that I cherished ordinary

ambitions and constraints as if only they were real. *Reality is
boundless, I vow to perceive it*— daily I chanted that vow

on my zafu, and while I struggled to embody whatever it meant
you simply *received* it, each day slipping into you with the easy

grace that occurs when one no longer has to think about it—one
is it. More directly, like oxygen, I received the words that tumbled

from you one afternoon years later, the last week
of your life, although I didn't know it was last, nor did you speak

a word I recognized. And yet together, we managed. You knew
what you meant, and I was able to fathom tone and touch

as you held my head gently at rest on your shoulder. And you
smiled. You smiled as you spoke. Little did I know I was

receiving *you* in the spirit of those wordless words. And it was
better I didn't. I'd have hoarded the words, as if words were

all I had. I'd have striven to receive them, to write them down
as food and sunlight, wine and stars. Last night, when I awoke

in a dream that gathered family and friends, laughter, good
food and drink, suddenly you were here with me, wearing

the old brown jacket you loved. You held me close. I can still
smell your skin. In the dream we are happy, and we are sad—

"How is it?" I ask, and you smile. You know I mean the afterlife
whatever that is. "I don't know," you reply, saying the words

clearly, if quietly, the moment so real I go off to see if there's still left
on the table a piece of fruit pie. Apple. Or rhubarb. Your favorite . . .

WHAT HE KNEW

for David

◯

Before Alzheimer's

and during it when he spoke in stray words
or in sounds

he sometimes moved his hands
like birds
        in flight

So that, watching his hands
punctuate the air

I'd ask myself

Am I watching birds disappear? Or a flower, opening?

◯

"If we can say that language is *the house of being* . . ."
a friend begins

And because I don't know
I enter
        quietly

the house
each word is, looking for

the word inside the word

its sequestered
essence

Inside *beatitude*
        be

Inside *bless*
           less

○

Be less

And if illness is a spiritual path, he surrendered
loss by loss
           word by word

what he'd learned to construct, what he'd learned
to imagine
as a self

Does he still know you?
                    People liked to ask that question

○

There's a law in physics that says
Nothing is lost

The spiritual law that may correspond
is this—
           Not until everything is taken
           or surrendered

will we find out what remains

○

I remember, late in the illness
he saw

geese flying low along a river

and moved his arms
              as they their wings

his body
an inaudible shapeliness, his mind perhaps a mirror

Another way to say it, he was
word
       made flesh

○

A book falls open to these words—

Ultimate meaning is not a matter of language at all . . . in the Zen notion, words trace the ultimate as a flight of birds traces their course through the air,

That is, one might, if anything
say, *Ah!*
       a form of saying nothing

as bird cloud flight wing skein air
intermingle

even as they shine alone

○

Inside *notion*
        no

Inside *negate*
        gate

Inside *silence*
       a *lens*

○

In the nursing home one morning, doing nothing
waiting
        as sun turned the table gold

we were looking at the moth orchid on that table

how its shadow-flower made a rounded
pair of wings . . .
           we were studying

revelation by shadow, or I was—

when he reached for my hand and out of nowhere
fully awake and smiling

a nature ripened and innate
said

I'm sorry I said that to you

And although I had no way of knowing what he referred to
he knew
        and so I let

the moment be the golden flower
our lives
already are
          even when we are immersed in shadow

It's okay, I said, and we kissed
a moth's kiss, light
           and the moment folded its wings

and settled into being

THE GLASS GLOBE

Wanting to begin again, a form of denial, I copy from a book
rearranging the words with a shaking hand . . .

This morning from where I sit, the rug is dark blue and burgundy
brighter where a length of full sun from the east window falls

On the shelf of the bay window a large glass globe, hand blown
the color of air over the shallows of the Sound summer mornings

shimmers, it all but floats . . . This morning, glad of it, I'm not going
anywhere, content as the globe fills with the quiet simplicity of light

This glass globe—it's a made thing, a synthesis of sand and fire, air
and muscle and lung and tool, a flaring of energies joined

and transformed, and because of the quality of attention
that went into it, beautiful. And it rests in a precarious place

I have to move it as I open the windows. I shift it when I dust, and if
I'm not careful, my mood hard and angular, I may knock against it . . .

And this is history—
$\qquad\qquad$ this is prose. My prose, words

in a book now out of print, words underlined by my husband
whose hand now is ash in a wood-fired ceramic jar

Except for me, everyone who came to our wedding is
dead. I'm in another house now. The glass globe rests in another

morning's light. Each morning, I walk out of this house to stand
alone in the quiet of these woods, whose leaf-rumpled

earth, so long ago now, was cleared and planted, grazed, hayed
harvested, abandoned—before that, scraped clean

by the sharp edge of the glacier; before that, marsh and sediment
before that, shoal and sea depth; before that, stone. When I take

my shoes off, my bare feet touch granite that was here
before leafy decay and woods-earth formed. Now I stand on it

shaken—I've done it, the fault is mine. I remember a Chinese sage
holding up a ceramic bowl, smaller than the globe in my window

but beautiful (therefore, the same—everything that partakes
of beauty is the same) and this gentlest of sages smiled as

he said, "The bowl is already broken." And he meant, live with it
that way—
                    love it, love it crazed

and cracked, love it broken. Because everything, everything
already is. Broken. And—was it moments ago? Dusting, I lifted

the glass globe, and when, even gently, I set it down, it cracked . . .
despite generations of care and abuse, it cracked, now

two fault lines rising from the base nearly to the lip, and here's
the crazy miracle . . . it holds. It still holds. But do the math

estimate probability, run the numbers, then stand
here bare feet on raw granite, from which a whispered

certainty—"We're done for"—rises razor-thin through flesh and bone
then lodges, a splinter of glass, in my throat . . .

RIVERKEEPER

Wanting to be that place where inner and outer meet
this morning

I'm listening to the river inside, also to the river
out the window

river of sun and branch shadow, muskrat and mallard
heron, and the rattled cry of the kingfisher

Out there is a tree whose roots the river has washed
so often, the tree stretches

beyond itself, its spirit like mine, leaning out over the water
held

only by the poised astonishment of being here

This morning, listening to the river inside, I'm sinking
into a stillness where what can't be said

stirs beneath currents of image and memory
below strata of muons and quarks

now rushes, now hushes and pools

now casts a net of bright light
so loosely woven

there's a constellation afloat on the surface of the river
so still

       I can almost hear it weave in and out

interstellar, intercellular ... and isn't it truly one world
no *in* or *out,* no *here* or *there*

seamless as a lily about to open

from just here into everywhere is. Just
is
    Restful lily. Lucky lily . . .

To bloom

must feel like a river's brightening at daylight
or a slow kiss
                  a throb in the elapse of time

a shudder of heron shadow flying over shallows
that are merely the apparent

skim of a depth whose bottomless surface seeps
everywhere

an anchored flow that upholds city and cathedral
bridge and gate

Orion, odd toad in the Amazon, blue dragonfly
what it is to love . . .
                  Spoil a river, you spoil all this

RESILIENCE

Right now there's a hum of bumblebees
fumbling
        in the plump, magenta

bridal bouquets
these blooms of rhododendron want to be

and I hum along, I hum along
until I see

how the black net, backgrounded
among the leaves
        snags and restrains

the blossoms—

like me, they're stymied, stalled
held back

and so, I choose patience
and scissors

and begin to snip
at the nearly invisible, insidious

black plastic netting thrown over
the bushes years back

to keep the deer off—one hard winter

they gorged on everything but stem
they ate each
        stellate spray of leaves

and all the tight buds

everything green that wasn't yet beneath
two feet of snow
                    or out of reach

and they left a band of emptiness
I could see through

all the next
summer and the next, until now the bushes
have healed—the words

spindly, stunted, broken down

fall away . . . but not
pinched, not *hunched,* these still apply . . .

so here I am fumbling, finally
cutting around the periphery of blooms

that, tight as fists or steepled picks
squeezed
                    their way

nearly through—I fumble and snip
pulling away
long, vertical shearings of net

trying not to hurry the work, not to tug

but shattering a few blooms anyway
as I strip away yards and yards of netting

then back to the scissors—

and it's no mystery how the mind
gets into it

how it knows, and complies with
a toss-up of
metaphor and memory—

take that earlier word,
                    bridal—

and now other words like *should*
and *you may not*

begin to shrivel at my feet, and the sun
heats my shoulders
                    as I lean further

into the work, and, oh yes, body
feels it, too
                    there's a quickening

to my step now, and when my shoulders
ache
and the muscles in my forearm go tense

I shake it off like rain

continuing strand by strand
lacuna by lacuna
                    to ruin

the nets I'd agreed to . . .

once upon a time, they had seemed the only way

But nothing
takes the place of this lifting up and up

of branches with their load of blooms
this springing
                    into the sunlit air

nothing's better than the invitation

to stretch, to rise and come into bloom
to rejoin
the commonwealth

of the pure and ravenous, lascivious
and riotous
being
             blossom is . . .

REFLECTION, LOOKING
STRAIGHT AHEAD

... this morning, I have to confess, mirrors
confuse me

especially the small one over the dresser
that faces
            the open bedroom door

so that, all this while, years really
brushing my hair
                choosing an earring

looking straight ahead

I haven't noticed that at least half
of the painting

over the sofa in the next room
floats
        in the mirror

a field and sky at sundown
right there

next to my face

I know that to *look* is one thing
to *see,* another

that it's more than a matter of angle
focus, stance—

but to think that all the while
I've been leaning in close

the painting has been there
field and sky

and noticing them now, finally
I'm drawn to consider

what else daily I live with
and don't notice

afraid to, perhaps . . .

As a child I'd drift into wondering
what if
           after the final

conflagration, erasure, rapture
or roiling upheaval

what if only I survive

how then would I find food or grow it
make a brick

understand gravity, list
the elements

solve an equation, sketch an atom
hum the whole of

Beethoven's Ninth
recall a wren—

and why must I pare myself down
to the last-one-left

before I admit the fields and the woods
already are silent
               as nearly

silent as they are in the painting
only partially

reflected in the mirror, where
next to my face

summer field and horizon
lie close

so close we share the same skin
the same

sun already gone down gold
behind dark cedars

leaving the sky

lit

the immense painted sky
drizzled
           with delicate

black smatter, with tiny motes
that fall on everything

equally, and I didn't notice them
before
           I didn't see them

until now here they are, falling
into a mirror
                in which

simply to see myself there
rouses the question

each breath of mine has tried
to conceal . . .
                why must I die?

GREED

Even the fox of legend knows
that inside *immortal*
is

    more

Extinction is a fox skin
that rots in the ravine behind the house

whose foundation
is eroding

Will you be spared? Will I?

What shall we mourn?

    a river

    a flower

    a tongue on the spiral galaxy of the body

    a peach

Add to that, the pain each of us has not
acknowledged

Were we less churlish and afraid
perhaps we might

investigate how long it takes to imagine

earth without us

How long to sever
the link

between *relish* and *ravish*

ASIDES AND NOTATIONS

quiddity: the essence, nature, or distinctive
peculiarity of a thing; that which answers
the question, *Quid est?*

NAME

Bloodroot, forsythia, phoebe

To name things
enacts our essence, so it's said

I'd rather the world turned
and named *me*

Stood face to face and whispered
so quietly

I'd have to lean close and ask, "Say again?"

PROPORTION

After years of practice, still I mistake

the moment's
heft

Whether it asks us to lift a pound of feathers

or let a feather
carry

in an updraft of breath

It is to mistake appetite

Epic, when a lyric morsel will do

COLOR AND SOUND

Sing, Muse, the hue of movement
also, its music

how a bird in flight

high over our heads
may be

flash of light and call note
combined—

so daring a display

that even the most eloquent
among us

(steeped
in difference and distinction)

might envy it

GRAMMAR

Given that language meddles
so intimately

with matter, we might want to

reevaluate each word we speak
right down to

the least particles of speech

no matter their origin or address

whether animate, archaic, foreign
casual, or intensive

asking each word, Do you invite

or exclude?

Let's start, for example, with *tu* . . .
vous . . . *this* . . . *thus* . . . *thee*

CLIMATE

Surely someone will devise
an isotherm

for grief, once the shearing-off
from ice sheets

in Antarctica and Greenland
erases coastal

wetlands cities rivers fields
and reservoirs—that is

when *elsewhere* is tangibly *here*
and we can taste it

flavoring the water for coffee once
served steaming

in outdoor cafes in what we remember
as Amsterdam

Cape Town, San Francisco, Rio

CONTEXT

On the path to Main Brook
far from Darfur

a flurry of snow
speckles the leaf-litter

and I see how a local painter
adapts

this wintry texture, these flecks
of color

to render human skin in his portraits
of widespread famine—

so that flesh is consensual
is mottled
    is earth

IMPERMANENCE

It will not always be someone else's death

SKY POND PLACE

○

Undercast and overcast, pond and sky, and both a tarnished silver
as, over and under
                    two goldfinch dip and rise

and now the wind lifts
                    then settles, first an outreach of pine bough
then oak
        then chestnut

only to shelter briefly in the hollow of my throat

○

A clearing in the sky, and this yard with its grassy slope in morning
      dew and sunlight, this yard

is a Chinese poet, Sung dynasty, writing in mist and air

○

As for vesture of dwelling: house, well, woodshed, stone bench
and a path away from it all

into the dense woods, whose ceiling is mottled, gaps of blue and
      dove-throat gray
                 and, yes

also my chair beginning to green in its shady corner, tucked back
      among fern and daylilies

○

It's just right now, the light . . .

so that one sees an afterthought of rain trembling from the tip of
        a peony leaf

as wind-stir
                billows out a web between two stalks

whose lilies once
were hallelujahs in the now silent morning

○

Mourning cloaks in the phlox, the lilting weight of petals falling

○

Oh, what if one were to
stay out all night
                        past moonrise into the river of stars

what if evening
soaks shirt and skin

what if
        the barred owl rows its heavy wings through the opening air

and its haunting call
scatters

the fragrance of the silvery phlox
and skims off
                each and every thought

what if

    watching the deer browse the chordate leaves of the violets
    and the hostas

and the roses

one sits quietly ... waiting
no

not even waiting

what if the angle of the moon traces
a path of light

onto the pond
 and in all this, what if

nothing in you holds back—all of it no other than yourself

○

Joined in the single sweep of a glance, neither pond nor sky
takes precedence—
 you can see how

clouds enter each one equally

Oh, what are we waiting for? There are water skimmers and lilies
 on the skin of a cloud—

time to go swimming in the sky...

Cloud Koan

What comes from nowhere and is inseparable from
the wind, the sky, the stones?

I've taken the vow of clarity—and still, the mind
that sly magician

does its sleight of hand

I lie down in the grass, or I walk the winding dirt lane
and it's not often I recall how

the ongoing *now you see me/now you don't*
of each blossom and leaf

is anchored

only to a thin crust that floats on molten slurry . . .
We call it *ground*—and from this

illusion of solidity

a host of metaphysical metaphors arise
and, often, sustain us. I clap my hands and seem

solid enough, but I'm a cloud in slow motion
like these overhead mountains of mist

bright white with freshly laundered sunlight
and blue gray shadows—these

caused, believe it or not

by residual dust. I watch clouds gather and mimic
the head of a dog, a whale . . .

then England and Asia Minor appear on a royal
blue sea of afternoon sky. My dog

right now rolls in the grass

he's so delighted, and I'm all for it, also flat
on my back in the thick grass

filled with delight and alarm

at the mind's gift for imputing meaning
into anything at hand. Never mind

if I don't understand. Never mind that in the midst
of all this celebration, I'm the illusion

that thinks *I'm alone,* alone and still married
to the house which once

anchored us, its roofline against the sky
so solid-seeming even now, it makes

the unending blue of the sky

even more blue—a color concocted by sunlight's
scattering itself

near the violet end of the spectrum, into which
I'm drifting . . .

Nor have I answered the question

SOLVING FOR THE ROOT

Weeding, as I am now
words occur
        equation . . . elegance . . .

No boundaries
between
        what wanders into the mind

and the wild onions in the periwinkle
the ferns in the lilies

Who's at home here?

I awoke this morning wanting to solve for the root of the infinite

and have settled for
the notion

that the wild garden of the world is
its own
        mute and unknowable

statement, as is Chartres, as is a trilobite

as is the seed syllable, ruby-throated
nearly audible
        in the wing whir of a hummingbird that chances by

An interpreted world is not a home
said
        Hildegarde de Bingen

who spent lifetimes moment by moment

in a silence and tangible mystery that goes
        deeper in
        and further
                    than mathematical

        proof, or lyric inference, might suggest

        She had her prayer beads

        I, this kneeling mat
        this trowel

BUTTERNUT SQUASH
HEART SUTRA

Overwintering
in the cool of the root cellar
not stained, not pure
neither waxing nor waning
its once ripened
succulence
gone dry, it has hollowed
from the inside out
as if a ball of clay
has been thrown onto a cosmic wheel that spins by itself
offering us
form as emptiness, emptiness as form
and thus
it's cradle and coffin
it's a niche whittled into a cliff face by wind
a shrine
before which anyone might bow, *O Sariputra*
and because there is
no old age and death
no cessation of old age and death
when I balance it on my palm
it's the carapace
of a dung beetle's journey
achingly slow
it's a turtle shell
faded to colors of saffron and cinnamon
that swirl
around its own
oval emptiness, it's a patchwork
of textures
in part wrinkled
raincoat and satin cloak
in part a dun-colored
shale, very like my own skin
so that where the stem
broke off

at that point of rupture, now I rest
one finger
and because everything that is
is mercifully
plural
right here now I sit down with the universe as it pulses, I sit
until words are
simply sounds
no one wishes to translate, and wish
is an energy
curved like time and space
each one of us
wrapped in sunlit garden soil, in riverbeds of night sky and stars
so that what used to be
wind
now is breath unfurling
in a boundless planetary sigh . . .

Gate, Gate, Paragate, Parasamgate, Bodhi Svaha!

WHITE PHLOX

○

Always too soon, shattering, the phlox from momentary
fullness
         scatters to never-more

their soft meticulous florets—it's their contract with entropy, perhaps

unsigned

○

And yes, and no, it's only the phlox that seem to scatter summer
and not us
         not us gathered in our charades and chorales

not us
     who also are
             unsorted ephemera in the ongoing retreat

Well, one learns to savor each tinctured shade of snow

○

Augmenting brevity, suppose they could speak? Why, one would be
struck dumb
        by their first mute syllable

whatever it is
        whatever it might mean
               Oh, and

they do speak! they do, if one listens with the whole of one's body

to the whole of theirs

○

Radiant, decorous gists

phlox are everything less than heroic, they are meek, uncertain poverties
having felt
     sooner than most, a downward tug at the base of their stems:

enough now
    enough of you

and your hillocks of froth, lush Appalachian composites of breath

each prim floret
having opened from retracted immensity and wilderness sinuosity

○

Nonetheless, a collective insistence on a fragrance

that billows
    as it dissolves

into vestiges played by no one other than the wind. . .

LIKE SO MUCH WEATHER

Like so much weather
the congregate mist of atoms I am

sits upright
         almost legible

Wind rises
vanishes
      returns

sunlight slants into the pines

And look—whoever breathes
now

lifts and settles
onto a branch and preens

whoever breathes now

shifts
revolves
opens
     brightens
     spindles
     scatters

resolves

now scrambles down the trunk
now scratches in the soft mossy dirt
now calls
        whooree in the oak grove

I am hunger
I am the relief of hunger

I empty and fill
                I am sent out anew

now spilling into shallows
into furrows
and ruts
and potholes

now rain, now snow

and I harden
shatter
melt back to mud

tighten
into pebble

whirl away
as dust

        become galaxy
        become genome

Look, I have just turned over in bed
gathered you
           released you

made a noise
said a word

fallen through the fathomless

become cloud

become shell
scale
skin
feather

fur

become a morning trill
                        a happy wag

a breach
a rolling current
a refuge
a slither

become whine
            burn
            delve
            dandle
            swerve

become thrust
and turn

merge
and praise

fall down
            and praise

Yes, praise

black fields
and green fields
                        they shine equally

And dying, as we do

into all this confluence

this commonwealth

this common life
arriving

          moment by moment

breath by breath, is

continuing
is
    going on . . .

isn't it?

BECAUSE THE EARTH

Because the earth as we know it will end
I plant dahlias

And because dahlias will fade, in late fall

I dig up their roots to make a potion that dyes
my scarf
of white silk

the color of the earth

And because the scarf will wear out
and will shred

I untie it from around my neck
off it flies
              into the wind with the prayer flags

And because my neck
will someday not be needed to hold up my head

I take down a recipe for stock
good bone broth

And because my head takes stock
of each leaf
as it settles

onto the dark shining surface of the pond

I reach for an invisible spool of red cord
knot the cord
and begin

mending the net we've torn

this net made of air and ocean, made of sun
and soil

At junctures, woven into this net
are jewels

whose each facet reflects star-groves and owls
minnows and eelgrass

meadow larks, milkweed, and monarchs

so that each apparently single
thing
        exists

in the light of everything else

And because the net also trembles

as it senses the glacial erratic
in any heart

that just sits there and sits there and sits there
a mute
        lament

and because each of us has the power to turn
harm
into healing

and because the earth as we know it will end

just now, I plant dahlias

EXCHANGE

a letter to David

Now that you've entered the great silence
I search out your scribbled notes and drafts

the remains of your work-in-progress
Each word I say aloud, drawing each one

into my body as if body were a vault
for *treasure*—a word you used to say with

a long *a. Treasure, pleasure, measure*—
I echo your odd torque of the vowel

Had your luck been otherwise, those words
would have been forged by you into memoir

and genealogy, your life a well-made
volume of breath. And so I gather

the scraps, piece by piece. I try to finish
your sentences, I forage through files

and boxes, I nose about for treasure
as do the midwinter deer outside in a year

the oaks put out few acorns. I'd eat
the bark off a pine if I thought I'd find

beneath its tight inscrutable cover
a trace of your voice. I want to get through

winter, too—I'm simply an animal who
feeds on words, finding yours spilling into margins

balanced steeply on underlinings
many more crossed out in your rough-hewn drafts

I savor the words, listening for your voice
in a continuous, if tenuous, exchange . . .

I see it everywhere, exchange—nothing's finished
I breathe out carbon dioxide, the summer oaks

take it in along with the sun, the leaves
power up, unfurl more leaves, give out oxygen

those doubled molecules I breathe in and in
without thinking much about it, but for

an occasional burst of gratitude
the sheer luck of being alive. *Sheer* . . .

A word so transparent, it might house spirit
the spirit I'd say, if I could make out

what it is. Up late, we'd often talk for hours
about a single word, a spirited exchange—

who knew where it would take us? And words
kept us close. But *sheer*'s partner is

stark, and together they make and unmake
treasure, pleasure, measure. What stays?

Firewood is a moment of *being time,* ash
also. Being time, we are like the shavings

that curled from the oak you planed into planks
to frame this house and lay the floors

Being time, we are whatever it is in us arises
meets, and merges into everything else . . .

Over the phone last night, your daughter
read me a letter you'd written her, found

tucked away in an old cardboard box
in the basement. Its subject: *How many*

can we invite to the wedding? A question
of some urgency back then. A time of *treasure*

pleasure, measure. Hungrily, I listened
to your words in her voice. Gentle words, and

wise, as you traced in an eloquent narrative
your passage in time through hardship to an

exchange of love no numbers can tally. That was
a moment. That was a meeting . . .

Perhaps a life's work is just this moment
just this much, breath shaped and released

given freely into the clear light . . . *How many*
can we invite to the wedding? All of it

is wedding—an exchange of words and sunlight
a moment of bud and blossom begun

in a rustle of leaves, a never-before-now
utterance suspended in sheer daring

the words shining, briefly held by who knows
what, before being swept once more

syllable by syllable, vowel by vowel
beyond the passion to endure, beyond

the passion not to be lonely, beyond
beyond, into the full and everlasting furl of silence

WING

○

How it was severed, or if it was sheared off
I don't know—
                nor

how long it lay in the path the mower had
already made

through the thick field of tall grasses, chicory
and thistle

But if the body, as it rots, loosens its bindings
and its grasp

                if it opens its sheath

then perhaps my neighbor, who chanced upon it
simply lifted the owl

by one wing, and the rest of it, the core, fell away

as a ripened fruit falls to earth when it's ready

○

I have learned to listen to the word inside a word
as if it is
                the whisper I need to hear

Inside *flower*
          flow

inside *seclusion*
             clue

inside *heart*
           the *art* of listening

○

All winter, while the one wing
aired in the woodshed

and the lingering odor
faded
      I kept silent

until, inside *not knowing*

a *wing*

began to rustle
began to throb
         began to stir

○

I had a friend who believed in not knowing
so deeply
      he understood

the *lie* inside *believe*

the *pin* in *happiness*
      the suffering in *paragon*

And yet he believed
his body
      had betrayed him—one illness, then

another, his body only falling
apart—
      he believed that, and he wanted

off the waterwheel
that turns the river of life, he wanted

to be washed into a sea of transcendent
love

○

Want, want, want

Who is this who wants, he'd ask—and, almost
I hear his voice

and the mute pain of that question

now as I walk
                        wing in hand

to a bench that overlooks the still pond, only weeks
after his leap

onto the rocks and into the river that flows
beyond the Sound and into the ocean

into deep night's white river of stars

○

Almost, I hear his lost voice

But as I place
                        the owl's wing

quietly onto the wooden bench and sit
beside it

what's more near
                        is a loud cry—

a live owl's pitch-perfect
call

absolutely single

its one syllable
not lengthy
            not lingering

no chuckles, no chortles, no mating duet
no lament
            no—

a clipped, strident

Whoo

○

And after, in the shock of silence, I know I am
held

in a gaze as bright, as brown
as pond water when the sun falls through

○

When a mind
in stillness
            looks out and in one glance takes in

the one
wing
        what does it see?

Who sees?

If I say
        here is a wing

designed for flight, and beautifully
made

its leading edge of feathers

notched for silence in the night air as the owl
swoops
to its prey

a wing wholly mottled and speckled
so that, camouflaged

in daylight
        it dwells nowhere among the trees—

do I also
dwell nowhere and come forth from that place

And if I say, or think, or suppose *I do,* have I not
opened
        a chasm to fall through

○

I stroke the owl's wing gently, with one finger

○

And yes . . . I will seize on words, I will fall

silently on them

and hold them down in a steady grasp
and open them

I will feed this hunger to know that inside

know
      is *now*

and that, lifting and falling, already it's flown to

the source
it never left

○

And when, each morning, I bow

I bow to the one wing of the river
                              to the one wing of the field

to whatever it is in us
sees through arising and passing ...

To that, I bow

JUDGE NOT

From inside the house, I hear
over by the woodshed

the steady sound of a maul
as it thwunks down
and splits

a chunk of oak, again and again
a muffled

heartbeat sound—

and I get it, how judging one another
works

the analytical split
it makes

how irrevocable the cleaving

and even if the split makes
cordwood
possible

there's also fire to come, and smoke
a toxic residue

in the air around each word I speak out
or imply in judgment

A suicide may leap free of another's
judging
and fall into

the mystery of the human heart

But what if it's common sense
what if it's clear

what if even a child, or especially a child

would say
          Stop!

How to do it, how hold
in balance

what misses the mark
and what hits it

How know without censure

how see the open wound
and the salt already in it

and refuse
to add a pinch more

And there's this enigma—
the heart

seems to need to be split
by error
even shattered

I'm only human
one may say, and I might say that, too

We might stand in a human chorus
and mutter it, over and over

But how put a stop to what harms
how make whole

how raise the maul and bring it down
and make

a break so clean one can

(reaching beyond what can or can't
be known)

touch what is . . .

NEVER PITILESS ENOUGH OR KIND

Nothing now you can do about it
you will be torn
from your bed, or you will
rise from the bare floor
of the shopping mall
from the factory's concrete
from the dirt road
where your car has stalled
and you will run, you will
flee in a panic, following
the last of the birds
to the shore, to the sea
where you hope to escape
the flames, the explosions
the whirling ash

Your whole life, haven't you known it would come to this

howsoever you sought
to shield yourself, sheltering
in the family and its things
sheltering, if you were poor
in whatever was left
of your dignity
Your eyes were never pitiless
enough, nor kind enough
Your attention was
scattershot, you never
focused on the great matter
which now has ripened unavoidably

Ah, my dear, you never understood

Perhaps now, as you rise
out of what's left of your body
you may remember
how once, only a child

you held in both your hands
a tiny replica of the globe
a manufactured tin orb
tinted azure for oceans
and for the continents
bold territorial colors—
it was a toy, that replica, not

the self-creating, self-sustaining earth that had the power

beginning with a single cell
to make from implicate
intelligence
your lush, evolving curiosity
Even so, you had only to
hold it out on your palm
as if it were the last apple
or the first flower
and what did you do?

Ah, my dear, you did . . . this

THE KEEP

When the epoch we call the Anthropocene
is stored

in the keep of the Anima Mundi

when our civilizations
are compressed

into a geologic layer the width of a wine glass

there will yet be mountains in the distance
and, when
                the air eventually clears

also stars in the steep interludes

No birds—not even
their disembodied voices, and only a few clouds

left behind to tarry against a magenta
sky
      in recumbent shapes

that may resemble humans, then ferns
then colossal barnacles

No waterfalls, no rivers, root cellars, wrist bones
or lilies

No cantatas, no fugues. No murals. And not one
miniature portrait
                  inside a pendant locket

Without us, you ask, will there remain
anything
          unstifled, or evolving

into what we might call *beautiful?*
Perhaps ...

        if only detectable by the micro-lidded

facets that will stipple surfaces at night
when the wind

lets up ...
        An iridescence

not unlike what we now think of as *sentience*

WHEN EVERYTHING
BROKEN IS BROKEN

When everything broken is broken
there still is a lake
in the meetinghouse of the heart
from which snow geese lift
and fly off, return and settle
When everything broken
is broken, into mind
come cars at rush hour
and, moving slowly
in the opposite direction
single file alongside the traffic
four lions, focused
and calm
their footfall steady
When everything broken is
broken
   still the sun
lifts blaze-red
behind the narrow slate-blue slats
of low clouds, and when it
sinks, also blazing
red below the darker ridge, who can
resist whatever it is comes
next?
   When everything broken
is broken, there are
galaxies, dolphins
old hymnals, wild apples
and the high meadow where we
once lay down
above the blue meander
of a river, along whose banks
midnight sycamores
stark in the starlight
sway into the emptiness one is
when everything broken
is broken

For a time
we were storehouse
and magnet and the wide-awake
light in your eyes
when I stepped from the train, coming back
home
        where
in the meetinghouse of the heart
there is lake
and highway, sanctuary
and sangha, lions
and a circle in the sweet grass
whose heal-all hums with bees
When everything broken
is broken
        after long silence
a voice—whose is it
not mine, not yours—
stirs, then lifts and carries
the moment
back to a river of floating sunlit
shadows . . .
and the river is like a sentence
whose syntax has faded
to a holy ache of syllables and vowels
that run through
my fingers. And the words, I've forgotten
the words, all but
these, *wondrous love*
and the timbre
        interrogative, tender. . .

ONE HOUR

If you had one hour to live and could make only one
call, who would it be to, what would you say, and why are you
waiting?

Night, and I come up the hill toward the house
away from the pond
where the tree frogs are singing
Otherwise it's quiet, and before I reach
the yellow rectangular slabs of light
which the house windows, lit from within
cast onto the dark grass, I turn
and look up at the stars—
                           I know
where I am as accurately as any
astronomer who plots the position
of Deneb, that lighthouse up there
unreachable but for the delay
of light—one need only track
the prepositions I use, to pinpoint where
according to the graph in my mind
I am—
               but I have no idea where
you are, my displaced Beloved, perhaps
that's why I turn myself around and around
turning the way the tilting earth
shelterless in the night sky turns—
I suppose there's an aerial vantage point
from which the earth is visibly
whole. For me, the view is limited to
oak rim, pond, hill, this place
where if I had only one hour left
I wouldn't know in what direction
to call your name—

Oh, I don't know where
soon enough I will be going, only where
I am now, and for that great gift I bow down
I bow to this darkened plot of earth
you in particular loved and on which
we stayed awake together the whole of
one night, inside by the kitchen window
where we watched a lunar eclipse—
and what did it matter we could see
only the shadow of the earth's rim
then the earth sliding gradually, partially
across the moon—

                       you said ever so gently
It's good to be here, and *with you* . . .

STAR KOAN

What galaxy can you find that is left out of your body?

I have learned to sink into the river in my wrist
find
    a sky path

and follow it to where the winged horse

rests its hind hooves
on Aquarius

Is this where I was born?

When Orion glints through
the galactic space between the branches

of the wolf tree maple alongside the lane
I know briefly
        the depth of what I am

and, briefly, the magnitude of brightness
of each yellow leaf

as in a whoosh
the leaves fall upward, as sparks would, into the wind

Wind is breath

I find Rigel in my left foot
Canis Major
      on the leash I hold

The mote in my eye is Arcturus
the dirt beneath my toenails

galactic dust

Given earth tilt
and the aberration of light

I need tether, and yet what joy there is
touching the edge
                    of the edgeless

Meanwhile, I know in my bones
how to live
                how to die ...

THIS MORNING

The green tea in my cup this morning
is bitter. I could go back to the kitchen
for honey—
             I could do that
but the moment hurts in a way that also
offers pleasure. What's that all about?

I've just lit the candle that once burned
on a table set with flowers, your photograph
your ashes
             And if I still
catch my breath when the flame shimmers up
I'm careful to let my breath out slow

Watch—I don't blow it out, and this ceaseless

flow of fire is now on the dresser in my bedroom
along with the Buddha I brought to that
scrap of
             home-away-from-home
I managed to create from family photographs
books, blankets, and music that calmed

your spirit—Japanese flute, Appalachian folk

There, out the window beside your single bed
a single maple
stood in
             for the woods outside
the bedroom window here, where just
this moment, passing by, I'm stopped

by a brightness that seems out of place

Out there, east end of the pond, floats a round
wavering sun in black water
The sun's in the water
                              and it doesn't get wet
The sun's also rising gold
through the matchstick winter trees

toward clear sky—no smoke, no conflagration
no regrets. I don't know how, but
the web of the screen
                              creates a vertical
shimmer of light, a plumb line that connects
sun above, sun below

And I bow—
                    how many years

how many, have I lived here and not seen this
precise, seasonal
miracle
             yoke sunrise and sun-depth
apex and abyss? Today, it seems
I'm keeping an old appointment with the sun

Perhaps I shouldn't be happy. But I am . . .

TIGER, TIGER

> The tiger fears the human heart. The human
> fears the tiger's kindness.
> —Korean koan

When I die, I'd rather not have

slipped on the slate walk one winter moment, in the dark
alone, and with no one in reach of my voice

Lying there, going gradually numb, only awake
because of the searing pain that won't let me stand on my own

will I offer myself calmly to the unknown? Will there be
stars in which to lose myself?

If this is one way to die, there are others equally as steep

It is possible not to be afraid of being afraid. It is possible
to be returned to a moment

one regrets, the voice sharp, heart brusque, and this time
stand still when the tiger springs, this time

smile into the tiger's eyes and let the entire universe of
precarious bounty sweep in. It is possible

to be intimate. To be kind . . .

INTIMACY

At the rim of the pond, there's a slim
blow-down, a sapling
pitched over
by a rainstorm that shattered
any surface reflection
It leafed out anyway, and its
flowers, small as dust motes
smell of nutmeg
married to the whiff of a memory
I can't quite place
Never mind its being pitched
into the pond, it's tethered
by the rescue lines of two slim roots
that burrow into the muck
so that the tree continues to feed on
the dark underneath
of mess and rot and ruin, to which
its own falling petals contribute
Today I stood beside it, at the edge
of pond water popping with pollywogs
and swift blue dragonflies—
no longer wondering if I had
rope enough, and muscle enough
to pull it out. No longer
thinking, I was so still a billow
of smoky pollen from the pines
blew through me
and a water snake poked
its shiny black and delicate head
through last year's sallow reeds
and after I don't know how long
when I looked up overhead
wings outstretched a red-tailed hawk

circle by rising circle was
being carried on a thermal, up and up
and so tenderly, far beyond any
conclusion I know how to make . . .

GRACE

In the endlessly present tense
of memory

now harried by joy, and in a hurry

I arrive at the nursing home, intent on taking him out
to the ocean overlook
or to lunch
   a change of scene

and I'm making things ready, making it happen

when, from within a measureless quiet
without looking up
he says
   Can you just sit with me?

And so, a steep pause . . .

in which, but for the unspoken
presence of death
there is little danger, or drama

And then I sit with him in a solitude that expands
breath by breath
to receive

all of us, whoever has been left alone in the dark

whoever, lost in a crowd of others, takes the hand
of a stranger
if it's offered

sometimes even if it's not

ALWAYS AN IMMIGRANT

Always an immigrant
the heart
crosses borders
and boundaries
it trespasses
it will not be held back
Windswept, sea-swept
star-swept
it is poor, porous
permeable
it is outcry and
prayer
and a murmur
that ends with
a question mark
Tell me, is it
inside you
the immigrant heart? Or are you
inside it?
I only know
it contains multitudes
this heart
whose color
is not
red or black, or brown
or yellow, or
white—
the immigrant
heart is
transparent
there is a light inside it, it fuels
galaxies
nurses a child
holds your beloved

as he sinks over
his last threshold
a thread of gold light
just visible
along the border
of his body
Just look, the immigrant
heart
races naked along the tide line
kisses
both bandage and wound
holds a cup
to the mouth that thirsts
and the cup runneth over
it leaps with the suicide
into the waterfall river
carries schoolbooks
and ladders
and songs
it translates
the law, and transforms it
this heart
in the heart of the world
brings the children out of
cages, crates
and sealed truck-beds
What is it, you ask, *What is*
this immigrant
heart
if not sweat
if not nectar
if not salt
if not aloe
            if not what the sages

have promised, the sages
in their desert hovels
and prison cells
the sages on the street corners
and in the subway
turnstiles
They know how the immigrant
heart
gives from its own boundless
mercy
and light, crossing into
beatitude
and bliss, into pain
and rejection
this heart a new life always arriving
your body, my body
one body in the makeshift shelters
we call our lives

IRREVOCABLE

○

Someone no longer alive

is hovering over a great expanse of smartweed, panic grass, and midden
where a house used to be
                    where trees and gardens once flourished

where puddles and ponds held a sky of clouds and stars
in place
        for a moment

and you lived there . . . Ah, my dear

○

I speak from the liminal space where your beloved's last barely audible breath
        slipped into your body

then out the window into the winter chill, whose horizon line it rolled up as if
        it was twine

into a point, a still point—
                 a full stop that opens the heart

From that point, I speak

○

As once you washed the body of your beloved
let us wash
        for the last time

this one earth, this only, and only once, for once and for all

earth
        as if it were a lover who has died, and we, not knowing what to do

at last must wash the poles, north and south

where long ago the ice

cracked open
                    sheared off
                              and melted
Last, the mountain peaks

Last, the crowns of oaks and maples, on whose bare branches long strips of torn
          plastic flutter

Also the steeples, the turrets, the domes

Last, the open fields and meadows, wash them clean

the vast desert and its last oasis

riverbeds and shrunken rills

ravines and gullies

the rocky promontories from which we viewed the sea
as it rose to cover the cities
                              Last, the cities

submerged full fathom or in low tide only the towers and the tips of the high-rises
          winking up

Last, the sidewalks, shop windows, market stalls

Last, pebble, shell, and skull

Last, lark

and satellite, wash them, and the field of broken mirrors

Last, the house

Last, the bed

Last, the hills of midden, and their treasures

a button

a seed

a feather

a zipper

a chip of china plate

Last, the nose cone, the black box

Last, the trawler, the landing gear, the microchip, the missing part

Last the kiva, the sweat lodge, the drum

Last, the prayer rugs, the pews, the cushions

Last, the seat of enlightenment beneath what remains of the small tree's spreading
canopy

Last, the factories, the foundries, the mills

the maze of subway tunnels

the turnstiles

Last, the eye of the needle through which we could not pass

Last, a gun, a mine, a missile

Last, a bridge

Last, middle C on the piano, last a cello, a violoncello, in particular the Sonata
for Violoncello no. 2 in D, op. 64, by Heinrich von Herzogenberg

precious because it was the last music you listened to

precious because, like the last word your beloved spoke, you did not know it was
	last

Last, the pattern of fish displayed on ice, and their many-eyed, one-eyed gaze

Last, the last whale beached on the shore at Truro

Last, the glint of an eye in the periwinkle, the lovely, sinuous ripple of a reclusive
	snake

Last, the chemicals, the vitamins, the pills, the chemicals

Last, a hearing aid

a pair of binoculars

a surgeon's knife, a sling, a robotic hand

Last, to list only a few from the multitude that perished, fox and laughing
	gull, swallowtail and hawk

lion panther coyote vole giraffe mosquito trillium hummingbird hibiscus owl

Last, the very last line in a poem by Rilke
the line
	you can't forget the ache of, the line you didn't enact, not one syllable

of it—
	You must change your life

○

Space, of course, lasts

I walk upon it, as one would walk on a tablecloth for a table no one will set

What's left of my eyesight has dimmed, what I hear is only wind
       and that, muted

And because I have nothing to write on, I build cairn after cairn, lifting stones

balancing them

touching what remains in place, as if it were a new alphabet, or a sentence in Braille

You are reading the last of the earth's last rivers and mountains—do you
       know that?

These stones, these silences

the last words

held in mind for a moment

as if they were a net of fireflies shimmering in a summer field one can't tell apart
       from a night sky and stars

Wash them
           each stone, each firefly

wash them clean

this one, a love cry

that one, lament

and the last one the wing of a warning you might still be able to hear

just as once, long ago
you caught the smoke of the oracle rising from a rift zone at the center of the earth

○

If these cairns, these stone syllables, survive, there may be no one left to read
   the poem they make—

           but if by chance, there is . . .

let the stones be read aloud, so that a human voice

might widen its reach, floating off among the stars like the ringing-through
   of a great bronze bell

like the audible layers of birdsong gradually moving west as dawn
brightens, or used to

and the great earth turns

Notes

"Panang Curry with Shrimp and Gustav Sobin:" The lines beginning with "like so much weather" are from Gustav Sobin's poem "Toward the Blanched Alphabets." The lines beginning with "wafted, now, on . . ." are from Sobin's poem "The Archaeologist: A Broken Dictation." Both poems appear in the anthology *The Wilds of Poetry*, edited by David Hinton.

"Grief and the Art of Archery:" Quotations are from *Zen in the Art of Archery* by Eugen Herrigel.

"Mountain Koan:" "a poem as much like granite as it can be" echoes Ezra Pound. This and the other "koan" poems are inspired by passages in Susan Murphy's lucid book *Red Thread Zen*.

"What He Knew:" The extended quotation is from the introduction of John P. Keenan's *The Gospel of Mark: a Mahayana Reading*.

"The Glass Globe" incorporates passages from an essay I wrote titled "The Glass Globe" in *Beneath a Single Moon*, edited by Kent Johnson and Craig Paulenich.

"When Everything Broken is Broken:" The title is from a line in "Faint Music" in Robert Hass's *Sun Under Wood*.

"One Hour:" The author of the epigraph is Stephen Levine.

CPSIA information can be obtained
at www.ICGtesting.com
Printed in the USA
LVHW091542020821
694314LV00004B/241